$1.00

A PETER
PAUPER
PRESS
BOOK

HAIKU HARVEST

JAPANESE HAIKU
SERIES IV

TRANSLATION BY
PETER BEILENSON
AND HARRY BEHN

DECORATIONS BY
JEFF HILL

THE PETER
PAUPER PRESS
MOUNT VERNON · NEW YORK

FOREWORD

OF ALL the *haiku* I have read — in English, since I know hardly a word of Japanese — the three previous collections from Peter Beilenson's press, and his pen, in my opinion are the best, by far the best, translations. He brought each picture to instant life. He did not cloud nuance with words. And yet each poem is fully at home in our own language. Each has its own inner music, with the least alteration of content, no forced sentiment or emotion, no mere cleverness. Tenderness, irony, exuberance, vision, a listening, and always beauty — he sensed in each of these qualities a dialogue between this world and the world of the spirit, and he conveyed both image and echo.

Having so admired his three books of over six hundred *haiku*, when asked to complete his fourth, I was hesitant. I could only try to do what he would have done. Following his way of work, I read all the translations I could find, recited Henderson's phonetic Japanese versions for sound, absorbed Atasaro Miyamori's literal couplets and his sensitive notes, finally bursting out with what seemed the inevitable; what I felt the poet might have said in English.

In doing this job reverently in Peter's stead, I am grateful for the pleasant company of his friends, Basho, Buson, Issa, Shiki, and others of those old Haijin who spoke with such beautiful, evocative simplicity.

This should have been Peter Beilenson's book. He had just come to Basho's joyous shout about bringing a snowball in by the fire, when he died.

Harry Behn

HAIKU HARVEST

JAPANESE HAIKU
SERIES IV

Snow whispering down
   all day long,
   earth has vanished
leaving only sky
                    JOSO

Dusk, adrift at sea...
   why look back
   at those lesser
hills hiding Fuji?
                    KIKAKU

Oh that summer moon!
   it made me go
   wandering
round the pond all night
                    BASHO

Chanting and humming
   gongs immerse
   the green valley
in cool waves of air
                    KYORAI

SO COLD ARE THE WAVES
   THE ROCKING GULL
   CAN SCARCELY
FOLD ITSELF TO SLEEP
                  BASHO

WHEN THE AUTUMN WIND
   SCATTERS PEONIES,
   A FEW
PETALS FALL IN PAIRS
                  BUSON

MY DEAR PILGRIM HAT,
   YOU MUST
   ACCOMPANY ME
TO VIEW THE PLUM TREES!
                  BASHO

HOW HOT AND DUSTY
   THESE SUNSTRUCK
   COBWEBS GLISTEN
BETWEEN DRY BRANCHES!
                  ONITSURA

TWICE PERHAPS THREE TIMES
   THE CHIMES OF THE RIVER
   CHANGED...
OH WHAT A COLD NIGHT!
                ROKWA

EYES, YOU HAVE SEEN ALL...
   COME BACK NOW,
   COME BACK TO THE WHITE
CHRYSANTHEMUM!
                ISSHO

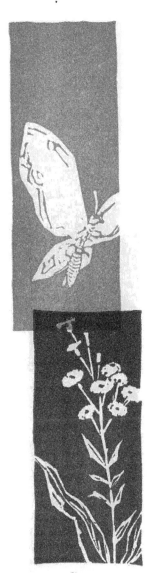

A CUCKOO CALLS
   AND SUDDENLY...
   THE BAMBOO GROVE
LIGHTED BY MOONBEAMS
                BASHO

ON THIS WELL-WORN STONE
   GARLANDED WITH
   PINKS OF SPRING...
O TO DRINK AND DOZE!
                BASHO

HE WHO CLIMBS THIS HILL
  OF FLOWERS
    FINDS HERE A SHRINE
TO THE KIND GODDESS
              BASHO

MOONLIT FLOWER-FIELD...
  DAYLIGHT GIVES IT
    BACK AGAIN
TO A COTTON FARM
             BASHO

IF I COULD BUNDLE
  FUJI'S BREEZES
    BACK TO TOWN...
WHAT A SOUVENIR!
             BASHO

HAVING SPOKEN ILL
  MY LIPS NOW
    FEEL THE COLD OF
AUTUMN'S FATAL WIND
             BASHO

SOME POOR VILLAGES
   LACK FRESH FISH
   OR FLOWERS...
ALL CAN SHARE THIS MOON
                SAIKAKU

UNKNOWINGLY HE
   GUIDED US
   OVER PATHLESS HILLS
WITH WISPS OF HAY
                BASHO

UNCHANGED BY AUTUMN'S
   ICY WINDS...
   THE CHESTNUT'S SHELL
STAYS GLEAMING GREEN
                BASHO

MY EYES FOLLOWING
   UNTIL THE BIRD
   WAS LOST AT SEA
FOUND A SMALL ISLAND
                BASHO

THAT WINTER WHEN MY
   FAITHLESS LOVER
   LEFT ME...
HOW COLD THE SNOW SEEMED
                    JAKUSHI

NO WONDER TODAY
   ALL THE MEN NEED
   MID-DAY NAPS...
O THAT AUTUMN MOON!
                    TEITOKU

CHERRY BLOSSOMS, YES
   THEY'RE BEAUTIFUL...
   BUT TONIGHT
DON'T MISS THE MOON!
                    SO-IN

AH THE FALLING SNOW...
   IMAGINE DANCING
   BUTTERFLIES FLITTING
THROUGH THE FLAKES!
                    OEHARU

THIS OLD HAT, STOLEN
   FROM A SCARE-CROW...
   HOW FIERCELY
THE COLD RAIN PELTS IT!
                KYOSHI

THE OAK TREE STANDS
   NOBLE ON THE HILL
   EVEN IN
CHERRY BLOSSOM TIME
                BASHO

POPPY PETALS FALL
   SOFTLY QUIETLY
   CALMLY
WHEN THEY ARE READY
                ETSUJIN

WHEN A NIGHTINGALE
   SANG OUT,
      THE SPARROW FLEW OFF
TO A FURTHER TREE
                JURIN

THE STILL SNOW WE
   WATCHED ... HAS IT
   COVERED THE SAME HILL
AGAIN THIS WINTER?
                  BASHO

UNDER A SPRING MIST,
   ICE AND WATER
   FORGETTING
THEIR OLD DIFFERENCE ...
                TEITOKU

IF MY GRUMBLING WIFE
   WERE STILL ALIVE
   I JUST MIGHT
ENJOY TONIGHT'S MOON
                 ISSA

UNMOVED, THE MELONS
   DON'T SEEM TO RECALL
   ONE DROP
OF LAST NIGHT'S DOWNPOUR
                  SODO

WHO CARES TO NOTICE
   CARROT FLOWERS,
   WHEN PLUM TREES
EXPLODE INTO BLOOM!
                SODO

DO THE TEA-PICKERS
   ALSO HIDDEN
   AMONG LEAVES
HEAR THE CUCKOO'S SONG?
                BASHO

IN MY SMALL VILLAGE
   EVEN THE FLIES
   AREN'T AFRAID
TO BITE A BIG MAN
                ISSA

OH THE FIRST SNOWFALL!
   WHO COULD STAY INDOORS
   ON SUCH
A GLORIOUS DAY!
                KIKAKU

IN STONY MOONLIGHT
   HILLS AND FIELDS
   ON EVERY SIDE
WHITE AND BALD AS EGGS ...
                    RANSETSU

WAKING BEFORE DAWN, SEE
   HOW THE CONSTELLATIONS
   ARE ALL
TURNED AROUND!
                    RANSETSU

AMONG THESE LOVELY
   CHERRY BLOOMS,
   A WOODPECKER
HUNTS FOR A DEAD TREE
                    JOSO

O THE TINY CRY
   OF A PITIFUL
   CRICKET
CAUGHT IN A HAWK'S BEAK!
                    RANSETSU

EVEN IN CASTLES
   I HAVE FELT
     THE SEARCHING BREATH
OF THE WINTRY WIND
             KYOROKU

EVEN I WHO HAVE
   NO LOVER...
     I LOVE THIS TIME
OF NEW KIMONOS
            ONITSURA

CUCKOO, DID YOU CRY
   TO FRIGHTEN AWAY
     MY MOTHER
WATCHING IN MY DREAM?
            KIKAKU

NOW THE DRAGONFLIES
   CEASE THEIR MAD
     GYRATIONS...
A THIN CRESCENT MOON
            KIKAKU

NEW YEAR DAWNING CLEAR...
   CHEERFUL SPARROWS
   CHATTER
ALL DAY LIKE PEOPLE
               RANSETSU

PINE TREE SILHOUETTE
   PAINTED BY THE
   HARVEST MOON
ON A SHINING SKY
               RANSETSU

WELL, THE FALL TYPHOON
   HAS TAKEN
   ITS FIRST VICTIM...
THE LOCAL SCARECROW
               KYOROKU

A LEAF IS FALLING...
   ALAS ALAS ANOTHER
   AND ANOTHER
FALLS
               RANSETSU

I'M VERY SORRY
   TO HAVE TO DIE
   AT THIS TIME
WITH PLUM TREES IN BLOOM
         RAIZAN

HOW CAN A CREATURE
   BE SO HATED
   AS A WINTER FLY
YET LIVE SO LONG!
         KIKAKU

POOR CRYING CRICKET
   PERHAPS
   YOUR LITTLE HUSBAND
WAS CAUGHT BY OUR CAT
         KIKAKU

EVEN THE GENERAL
   TOOK OFF HIS ARMOR
   TO GAZE
AT OUR PEONIES
         KIKAKU

EVERYTHING I TOUCH
 WITH TENDERNESS,
 ALAS
PRICKS LIKE A BRAMBLE
                ISSA

A YEAR HAS GONE BY
 AND STILL
 I'VE NOT YET LEARNED
MY NEW MASTER'S NAME
                RAIZAN

HELLO! LIGHT THE FIRE!
 I'LL BRING INSIDE
 A LOVELY
BRIGHT BALL OF SNOW!
                BASHO

A TRILL DESCENDING...
 BUT LOOK!
 THE SKYLARK WHO SINGS
THAT SONG HAS VANISHED
                AMPU

THINKING COMFORTABLE
　THOUGHTS
　　WITH A FRIEND IN SILENCE
IN THE COOL EVENING...
　　　　　　HYAKUCHI

THE SUN HAS GONE DOWN
　　BEYOND A DEAD TREE
　　CLUTCHING
AN OLD EAGLE'S NEST
　　　　　　BONCHO

SNOW SETTLED TILL DAWN
　　THEN CEASED...
　　NOW SNOWFLAKES GLITTER
ON TWIGS IN THE GROVE
　　　　　　ROKWA

WITH A WHISPERING HISS
　　THE SCARECROW'S STRAW
　　SCATTERS
AMONG THE STUBBLE
　　　　　　BONCHO

AN OLD SILENT POND...
INTO THE POND
A FROG JUMPS,
SPLASH! SILENCE AGAIN
BASHO

I MUST GO
   BEGGING FOR WATER...
  MORNING-GLORIES
HAVE CAPTURED MY WELL
CHIYO

WHERE DOES HE WANDER
  I WONDER,
   MY LITTLE ONE,
HUNTING DRAGONFLIES?
CHIYO

COOL GREEN GRASS...
  ONE DREAM ALL HEROES
  FIND TO BE TRUE
ON FORGOTTEN TOMBS
BASHO

WANDERING, DREAMING,
   IN FEVER
     DREAMING THAT DREAMS
FOREVER WANDER
               BASHO

THE SEED OF ALL SONG
   IS THE FARMER'S
     BUSY HUM
AS HE PLANTS HIS RICE
               BASHO

AUTUMN CRICKETS CRY,
   KOSAI THE POET
     IS DEAD,
HE NO LONGER SINGS
               KIKAKU

ANOTHER NEW YEAR
   AND MANY ANOTHER
     FLEDGLING
WITHOUT A NEST...
               ISSA

HOW COOL THE GREEN HAY
   SMELLS, CARRIED IN
     THROUGH THE FARM GATE
AT SUNRISE!
                 BONCHO

FAREWELL! LIKE A BEE
   RELUCTANT TO LEAVE
     THE SWEET DEEPS
OF A PEONY...
                 BASHO

HOME AGAIN!
   WHAT'S THIS?
     MY HESITANT CHERRY TREE
DECIDING TO BLOOM?
                 ISSA

THE DRAKE AND HIS WIFE
   PADDLING AMONG GREEN
     TUFTS OF GRASS
ARE PLAYING HOUSE
                 ISSA

WHEN SPRING IS GONE, NONE
   WILL SO GRUMPILY
   GRUMBLE
AS THESE CHIRPING FROGS
                    YAYU

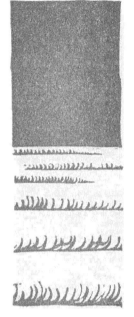

GAZING AT FALLING
   PETALS,
   A BABY ALMOST
LOOKS LIKE A BUDDHA
                  KUBUTSU

MY HORSE CLIP-CLOPPING
   OVER A FIELD...
   OH HO!
I'M PART OF THE PICTURE!
                    BASHO

HIGH ON A MOUNTAIN
   WE HEARD A SKYLARK
   SINGING FAINTLY
FAR BELOW...
                    BASHO

BEYOND PAPER WALLS
   VOICES OF GEISHAS
   WHISPER
ABOUT THE BRIGHT MOON
               BASHO

THE STEAMING RIVER
   HAS WASHED THE HOT
   ROUND RED SUN
DOWN UNDER THE SEA
               BASHO

SWALLOWS! THOSE HOMING
   BEES IN THE SUNSET
   BURDENED WITH HONEY,
SPARE THEM!
               BASHO

OVER THE RUINS
   OF A SHRINE,
   A CHESTNUT TREE
STILL LIFTS ITS CANDLES
               BASHO

IT IS NICE TO READ
   NEWS THAT OUR
   SPRING RAIN ALSO
VISITED YOUR TOWN
              ONITSURA

AT LAST, WHEN HER SONG
   IS STILL
   THE GODDESS BECOMES
A SMALL GREEN BIRD
              ONITSURA

A WIND-BELL TINKLING,
   HUSHED IN THE NOON SUN
   IS NOW
A SHELTER FOR BEES
              GONSUI

WHAT USE NOW ARE TWIGS
   BUT TO SWEEP UP
   A LITTER
OF FALLEN PETALS?
              BUSON

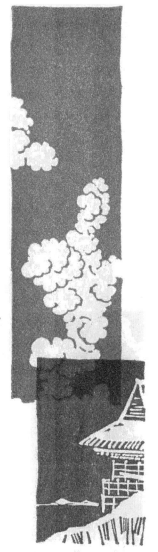

IN A WAYSIDE SHRINE,
   A HUNGRY OWL
     HOOTS AND HIDES,
SO BRIGHT IS THE MOON!
                  JOSO

ABOVE THE PILGRIMS
   CHANTING
     ON A MISTY ROAD
WILD GEESE ARE FLYING
              RANSETSU

ALL NIGHT THE RAGGED
   CLOUDS AND WIND
     HAD ONLY ONE
COMPANION...THE MOON
                BONCHO

HOW STILL IT IS!
   CICADAS
     BUZZING IN SUN
DRILLING INTO ROCK...
                BASHO

WE ROWED INTO FOG,
   AND OUT THROUGH FOG...
O HOW BLUE
HOW BRIGHT THE WIDE SEA!
           SHIKI

FROM WATCHING THE MOON
   I TURNED
   AND MY FRIENDLY OLD
SHADOW LED ME HOME
           SHIKI

WHEN MY CANARY
   ESCAPED, WELL
   THAT WAS THE END
OF SPRING IN MY HOUSE
           SHIKI

A VOICELESS FLOWER
   SPEAKS
   TO THE OBEDIENT
IN-LISTENING EAR
           ONITSURA

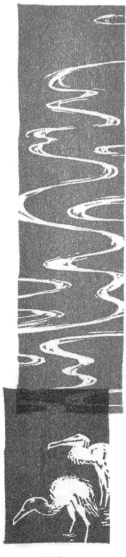

WITHOUT MY HAT! BAH!
  WHY DOES THIS RAIN
  HAVE TO PLOP ON MY PATE!
OH, WELL!
BASHO

BECAUSE SPRING HAS COME,
  THIS SMALL GRAY
  NAMELESS MOUNTAIN
IS HONORED BY MIST
BASHO

WAKE UP! WAKE UP! COME
  SLEEPY BUTTERFLY
  PLEASE JOIN ME
ON MY JOURNEY!
BASHO

LITTLE BIRD FLITTING,
  TWITTERING, TRYING
  TO FLY...
MY, AREN'T YOU BUSY!
BASHO

A SMALL HUNGRY CHILD
   TOLD TO GRIND RICE,
   INSTEAD
GAZES ON MOONLIGHT
               BASHO

WHAT BLOOM ON WHAT TREE
   YIELDS
   THIS IMPERCEPTIBLE
ESSENCE OF INCENSE?
             BASHO

PATIENCE, FROST!
   AFTER THESE FEW
   THERE WILL BE NO MORE
WHITE CHRYSANTHEMUMS
              OEMARU

HOP OUT OF MY WAY
   AND ALLOW ME PLEASE
   TO PLANT BAMBOOS,
MR. TOAD!
            CHORA

WASHING MY RICE HOE,
   RIPPLES FLOW AWAY...
  AS UP
FLY THE PIPING SNIPE!
                    BUSON

SPRING IS NEARLY GONE
   SO NOW
     THIS OLD CHERRY TREE
DECIDES TO BLOOM!
                    BUSON

FLOWERS IN SHADOW...
  A MOON FLOATING
   IN THE EAST,
IN THE WEST, THE SUN
                    BUSON

DAY DARKEN! FROGS SAY
  BY DAY... BRING LIGHT!
   LIGHT! THEY CRY
BY NIGHT. OLD GRUMBLERS!
                    BUSON

TIDES OF THE SPRING SEA,
    TIDE AFTER INDOLENT TIDE
    DRIFTING
ON AND ON . . .
               BUSON

BEYOND THE TEMPLE
    AND THE GARDEN LANTERNS,
    SWANS
AFLOAT AND ASLEEP . . .
               SHIKI

AS SHE WASHES RICE,
    HER SMILING FACE
    IS BRIEFLY
LIT BY A FIREFLY
               ANON.

A MOUNTAIN VILLAGE
    LOST IN SNOW . . .
    UNDER THE DRIFTS
A SOUND OF WATER
               SHIKI

ONE MAN AND ONE FLY
   BUZZING TOGETHER
   IN ONE BIG BARE
SUNNY ROOM ...
ISSA

WITHERED TUFTS OF GRASS ...
   ONCE UPON A TIME
   THERE WAS, AND IS,
AN OLD WITCH!
ISSA

SINCE I FIRST BECAME
   A HERMIT,
   THE FROGS HAVE SUNG
ONLY OF OLD AGE
ISSA

THERE GOES A BEGGAR
   NAKED
   EXCEPT FOR HIS ROBES
OF HEAVEN AND EARTH!
KIKAKU

OLD MAN WITH ONE EAR
   HELD CLOSE,
     DO I SOUND TO YOU
LIKE A BUZZING GNAT?
              ISSA

A SNOWY MOUNTAIN
   ECHOES IN THE
     JEWELED EYES
OF A DRAGONFLY
              ISSA

HEAVY WAVES CRASHING...
   SILENTLY
     OVER SADO
FLOWS HEAVEN'S RIVER
              BASHO

THIS IS MY OWN SNOW
   THAT SAGS
     MY OLD MATTED HAT,
AND IT'S LIGHT AS DOWN!
              KIKAKU

HAWKS OVER THE SEA...
   AS WE
     IN OUR VILLAGE DANCE
IN SMALLER CIRCLES
                TAIGI

WE COVER FRAGILE BONES
   IN OUR FESTIVE BEST
     TO VIEW
IMMORTAL FLOWERS
              ONITSURA

THE LEAVES NEVER KNOW
   WHICH LEAF
     WILL BE FIRST TO FALL...
DOES THE WIND KNOW?
              SOSEKI

MOON ADRIFT IN A CLOUD...
   I HAVE A MIND
     TO BORROW
A SMALL RIPE MELON
              SHIKI

PREACH AWAY, CRICKET,
   IT DOESN'T MATTER TO ME.
   I KNOW
IT'S AUTUMN
                SOSEKI

I MIGHT FEEL COOLER
   IF I WERE THE
   EMPEROR OF ROCKS
IN THE SEA
                SOSEKI

SINCE NO BELLS RESOUND
   IN THIS TOWN,
   WHAT DO PEOPLE DO
ON SPRING EVENINGS?
                BASHO

UNDER THE TEMPLE EAVES
   GOLD FADES...
   THROUGH BUDDING LEAVES
WE LOOK TOWARD THE PAST
                CHORA

WHOSE DRESS COULD THIS BE
   THIN ON THE LEAF-GOLD
   AUTUMN SCREEN?
ONLY THE WIND'S
               BUSON

ALL DAY IN GREY RAIN
   HOLLYHOCKS
   FOLLOW THE SUN'S
INVISIBLE ROAD
               BASHO

JEWELS OF SMALL SHELLS
   IN RIPPLES
   OF SAND, TANGLED
WITH KELP AND RUBBISH...
               BASHO

AFTER BELLS HAD RUNG
   AND WERE SILENT...
   FLOWERS CHIMED
A PEAL OF FRAGRANCE
               BASHO

BROWN LEAF FROM A TREE
   UNKNOWN CLINGS
     TO A STRANGE
GREEN-SPOTTED MUSHROOM
                BASHO

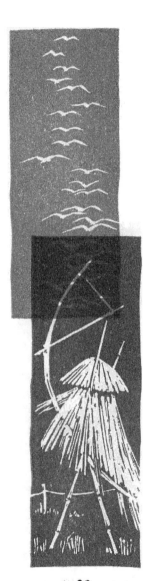

LIGHTNING FLICKERING
   WITHOUT SOUND...
     HOW FAR AWAY
THE NIGHT-HERON CRIES!
              BASHO

OUT OF ONE WINTRY
   TWIG, ONE BUD,
     ONE BLOSSOM'S WORTH
OF WARMTH AT LONG LAST!
              RANSETSU

BEHIND ME THE MOON
   BRUSHES
     SHADOWS OF PINE TREES
LIGHTLY ON THE FLOOR
            KIKAKU

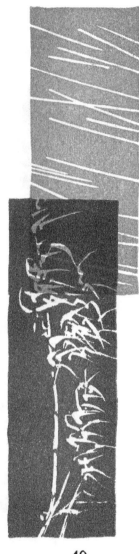

A NIGHT BRIGHT WITH STARS...
   WHOSE GHOST IS THIS
   WHISPERING:
SHALL I LIGHT THE LAMP?
                    ETSUJIN

RIPE HEADS OF BARLEY
   BENT DOWN BY A RAIN,
   BOWING
NARROW MY PATHWAY
                       JOSO

IT IS NOT EASY
   TO BE SURE WHICH END
   IS WHICH
OF A RESTING SNAIL
                    KYORAI

HO, FOR THE MAY RAINS!
   FROGS SWIM
   IN THROUGH MY OPEN
DOOR FOR A VISIT!
                    SANPU

AROUND THE GLOWING COALS
   OF A BRAZIER,
   OLD MEN TELL TALES
OF EARTHQUAKES
              KYOROKU

OH HOW I ENJOY
   EATING A RIPE PERSIMMON
   WHILE DEEP
OLD BELLS BOOM!
             SHIKI

FROG-SCHOOL COMPETING
   WITH LARK-SCHOOL
   SOFTLY AT DUSK
IN THE ART OF SONG...
            SHIKI

ONE PERFECT MOON
   AND THE UNCOUNTABLE
   STARS
DROWNED IN A GREEN SKY
            SHIKI

THE BEST I HAVE
   TO OFFER YOU
   IS THE SMALL SIZE
OF THE MOSQUITOES
BASHO

IF THINGS WERE BETTER
   FOR ME, FLIES,
   I'D INVITE YOU
TO SHARE MY SUPPER
ISSA

SLACK SAILS PUFFING FULL
   GLINT ON THE SEA
   IN A QUICK BRIGHT
WINTER SHOWER
KYORAI

UP FROM THE BOTTOM
   OF AN OLD POND,
   THAT DUCKLING
HAS SEEN SOMETHING STRANGE
JOSO

A THREE-DAY-OLD MOON
   ALREADY WARPED
   AND TWISTED
BY THE BITTER COLD!
                ISSA

AT DAWN MY CASTLE
   WAS STORMED
   BY A FLIGHT OF DUCKS
QUACKING IN A MIST
                KYOROKU

ONLY A CHIRPING
   INSECT TOLD ME
   IT WAS NIGHT,
SO BRIGHT WAS THE MOON
                ETSUJIN

NOT UNTIL I'D LOOKED
   A LONG TIME
   AT THE NEW SNOW
DID I WASH MY FACE
                ETSUJIN

SMALL BIRD FORGIVE ME,
  I'LL HEAR THE END
    OF YOUR SONG
IN SOME OTHER WORLD
                  ANON.

A RED LEAF FALLING,
  SETTLING
    INTO THE RIVER,
CLINGS TO A GREEN ROCK
                  JOSO

CALMLY FUJI STANDS
  HIGH ABOVE
    THE NEW LEAVES' WAVES
THAT BURY THE EARTH
                  BUSON

ON THE TEMPLE'S GREAT
  BRONZE BELL,
    A BUTTERFLY SLEEPS
IN THE NOON SUN
                  BUSON

WHAT A PRETTY KITE
   THE BEGGAR'S CHILDREN
   FLY HIGH
ABOVE THEIR HOVEL!
              ISSA

A CROW CLINGS SILENT
   TO A BARE BOUGH,
   CAUTIOUSLY
WATCHING THE SUNSET
             BASHO

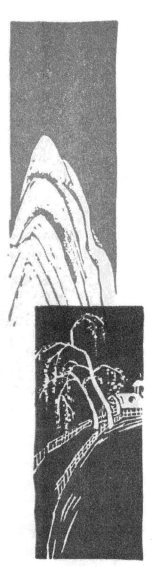

HOW FAR THE SKYLARK SOARS
   OVER
   A CLOUD-MOUNTAIN
BREATHING-IN SUN-MIST!
             SHIKI

IN THIS TOWN
   WHERE I WAS BORN,
   TONIGHT MY ONLY FRIENDS
ARE THE CRICKETS
             ANON.

DEFTLY THE NEW MOON
   BRUSHES
   A SILVER HAIKU
ON THE TIPS OF WAVES
                 KYOSHI

RAIN FALLING AT DUSK
   SWEPT ON, ON,
   SPILLING MILLIONS
OF MOONS ON GRASS-BLADES
                 SHO-U

CHANTING A PRAYER,
   MY HEART IS TWINED
   IN GARLANDS
OF MORNING-GLORIES
                 KYOROKU

SINCE MY HOUSE
   BURNED DOWN, I NOW OWN
   A BETTER VIEW
OF THE RISING MOON
                 MASAHIDE

SCARECROWS ARE THE FIRST
   HEROES TO FALL
   IN THE RUSH
OF THE AUTUMN WIND
                KYOROKU

BEANS FROM VINES
   GROWING OVER A
   SCARECROW
ARE EASY TO STEAL
              YAYU

SHAKING HIS LOOSE SKIN,
   A TIRED OLD HORSE
   SCARES AWAY
A WHITE BUTTERFLY
              ISSA

WHERE ARE MY NEIGHBORS?
   WHY DO THEY SEEM
   SO QUIET
THIS AUTUMN EVENING?
              BASHO

UNDER A FULL MOON
   ON A DISTANT
   TIDELESS SHORE
I HEAR MEN SHOUTING
            SHURIN

A POOL REFLECTING
   WHITE CLOUDS...
   DEEP IN A BAMBOO
SHADOW, A FISH STIRS
           SHURIN

WHAT DOES THIS MEAN?
   CHRYSANTHEMUMS
   AND JONQUILS
BLOOMING TOGETHER!
           SHURIN

BRIEFLY THE SUN SHINES
   BRIGHTLY BETWEEN
   CLOUD AND SEA
FADING AS RAIN FALLS
           ONTEI

WHEN THE TIGHT STRING
    SNAPPED, THE KITE FELL
    FLUTTERING...THEN...
IT LOST ITS SPIRIT
                    KUBONTA

IDLY, A SHIP GLIDES,
    THE TIP OF ITS SAIL
    DIPPING
THE POLISHED WATER
                    OTSUJI

INTO A COLD NIGHT
    I SPOKE ALOUD...
    BUT THE VOICE WAS
NO VOICE I KNEW
                    OTSUJI

CAREFULLY PUTTING
    HIS GOLDFISH BOWL
    ON THE PATH
HE RAN TO A FIRE
                    GESSHU

A HORSEFLY BUZZES
   LOUD
      IN THE SHINING HOLLOW
OF A TEMPLE BELL
               BOKUSUI

OVER THE WINTRY FOREST,
   WINDS HOWL
      IN A RAGE
WITH NO LEAVES TO BLOW
               SOSEKI

CUCKOO, IF YOU MUST,
   CRY TO THE MOON,
      NOT TO ME...
I'VE HEARD YOUR STORY
               SOSEKI

BUTTERFLY! THESE WORDS
   FROM MY BRUSH
      ARE NOT FLOWERS...
ONLY THEIR SHADOWS
               SOSEKI

THE MIGHTIEST GODS
   LOOM NAKED
   IN A BLACK WIND
LAUGHING AT DEMONS
                SOSEKI

A RAIN CLOUD DARKENS
   RED MAPLES
   CLINGING TO CRAGS
BY A WATERFALL
             SOSEKI

THE RIVER LEAPING
   ROCKS, ANGRILY
   ROARS AWAY...
AS THE MOUNTAIN SMILES
               MEISETSU

BROKEN AND BROKEN
   AGAIN ON THE SEA,
   THE MOON
SO EASILY MENDS
            CHOSU

EACH ELEGANT TREE
   HAS ITS OWN NAME...
THIS BEAUTY,
THE NIGHTINGALE'S ROOST
                   SOSEKI

DREAMING OF SHOUTING
   CICADAS,
   I WAKEN PARCHED
FROM MY NOONDAY NAP
                  SOSEKI

HONKING WILD GEESE COME
   SCRAWLING DELIGHT
   IN SPRING'S COLD
PALE MORNING SUNLIGHT
                   SOIN

BUTTERFLIES!
   BEWARE OF THE SHARP
   NEEDLES OF PINES
IN THIS GUSTY WIND!
                  SHUSEN

O MOON,
  WHY MUST YOU INSPIRE
  MY NEIGHBOR TO CHIRP
ALL NIGHT ON A FLUTE!
                KOYO

I KNEW FROM THE SOUND
  OF HIS TINKLING BELL
  A PRIEST WAS THERE
IN THE MIST
              MEISETSU

WATCHING THE SPRING MOON
  RISE,
  I NO LONGER BOTHER
ABOUT THE MOUNTAINS
                KYORAI

UNDER A HELMET
  HUNG IN A SHRINE,
  A CRICKET
CHIRPS HIS LAST COMMAND
                BASHO

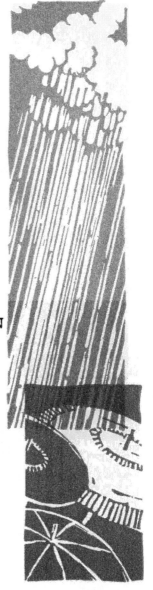

I CALLED OUT: WHO'S THERE?
　　WHOEVER IT WAS
　　IN SNOW
STILL KNOCKS AT MY GATE
　　　　　　KYORAI

BEYOND THE MOUNTAIN
　　I WATCHED A RAINBOW
　　PAINTING
THE SAGE'S VISION
　　　　　　MEISETSU

WHERE THE CUCKOO'S DARK
　　SONG CROSSES
　　THE SKYLARK'S CLEAR
HIGH SONG, THERE AM I!
　　　　　　KYORAI

THE SPEECH OF INSECTS
　　AND THE SPEECH OF MEN
　　ARE HEARD
WITH DIFFERENT EARS
　　　　　　SHIKI

A RED MOON GOES DOWN
    LATE IN THE WEST...
    SHADOWS FLOW EASTWARD
AND VANISH
                  BUSON

AFTER A SHOWER,
    THE CLEARING SKY
    SMELLS FAINTLY
OF HAWTHORNE BLOSSOMS
                  SHIKI

IN MY HOUSE THIS SPRING,
    TRUE, THERE IS NOTHING,
    THAT IS,
THERE IS EVERYTHING!
                  SODO

FOOLISH DUCKS,
    YOU KNOW MY REEDY POND
    IS OLD AND
WATCHED BY A WEASEL!
                  BUSON

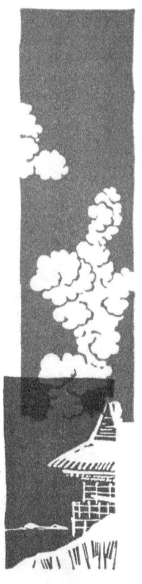

WILD GEESE HAVE EATEN
   ALL OF MY BARLEY...
   ALAS,
THEY ARE FLYING ON!
                  YASUI

OVER THE DEEPEST
   DARKEST RIVER,
   THE FIREFLIES
ARE FLOWING SLOWLY
                  SHIYO

AS FROGLETS
   THEY SANG LIKE BIRDS...
   NOW SUMMER IS GONE
THEY BARK LIKE OLD DOGS
                  ONITSURA

THE SLIGHTEST BREEZE
   BLOWS AND THE SKY'S DRY
   SHELL IS FILLED
WITH THE VOICE OF PINES
                  ONITSURA

COME COME! I CALL.
   BUT THE FIREFLIES
   FLASH AWAY
INTO THE DARKNESS
          ONITSURA

WARBLER IN MY PLUM TREE,
   PERCHING THERE
   IS AN OLD
CUSTOM OF YOUR CLAN
          ONITSURA

EVEN STONES IN STREAMS
   OF MOUNTAIN WATER
   COMPOSE
SONGS TO WILD CHERRIES
          ONITSURA

AT LAST! IN SUNSHINE
   SPARROWS
   ARE BATHING IN SAND,
FLUFFING THEIR FEATHERS
          ONITSURA

A TREE FROG SOFTLY
   BEGINS TO TRILL
   AS RAIN DROPS
SPATTER THE NEW LEAVES
                  ROGETSU

A DRIFT OF ASHES
   FROM A BURNED FIELD,
   A WAILING
WIND SIGHING AWAY...
                  ONITSURA

WHAT A SPLENDID DAY!
   NO ONE IN ALL
   THE VILLAGE
DOING ANYTHING!
                  SHIKI

WHY DO THEY WANDER
   OVER THE GREEN HILLS
   IN SPRING?
WHY DO THEY COME HOME?
                  SHIKI

BEYOND A DARK WOOD
   LIGHTNING REVEALED
   STILL WATER,
BRIGHT, LIKE A VISION
                 SHIKI

IF THE WHITE HERONS
   HAD NO VOICE
   THEY WOULD BE LOST
IN THE MORNING SNOW
                CHIYO

LEAF FALLING ON LEAF,
   ON PILED-UP LEAVES...
   RAIN SPLASHING
IN POOLS OF RAIN...
                GYODAI

ENVIABLE LEAVES,
   BECOMING
   SO BEAUTIFUL
JUST BEFORE FALLING...
                SHIKI

LIGHTNING FLASHING
    ALL NIGHT IN THE EAST
    THIS MORNING
SMOULDERS IN THE WEST
              KIKAKU

THE ROOSTER, FIGHTING,
    SPREADING
    HIS RUFF OF FEATHERS,
THINKS HE'S A LION!
             KIKAKU

A BABY WARBLER GAILY
    SWINGING
    UPSIDE-DOWN
SINGS HIS FIRST SONG!
             KIKAKU

YOU FLEAS SEEM TO FIND
    THE NIGHT AS LONG
    AS I DO.
ARE YOU LONELY, TOO?
              ISSA

THE SEA THIS AUTUMN
　　EVENING IS GREEN,
　　THE RICE FIELD
IS GREEN AS THE SKY
　　　　　　　BASHO

WELL! HELLO DOWN THERE,
　　FRIEND SNAIL!
　　WHEN DID YOU ARRIVE
IN SUCH A HURRY?
　　　　　　　ISSA

AS MOUNTAIN SHADOWS
　　DARKEN MY GATE,
　　THE TEMPLE DEER
STILL SEE SUN-RAYS
　　　　　　　BUSON

HE IS UNKNOWN,
　　THE POET WHO SINGS
　　THIS GREATEST
OF ALL SONGS — SPRING!
　　　　　　　SHIKI

CPSIA information can be obtained
at www.ICGtesting.com
Printed in the USA
BVHW031222280722
643247BV00015B/879